The
Carib-Asian
Cookery Book

Recipes and Rhymes

Sherrie Eugene-Hart and Patrick Hart

SilverWood

Published in 2016 by SilverWood Books

SilverWood Books Ltd
14 Small Street, Bristol, BS1 1DE, United Kingdom
www.silverwoodbooks.co.uk

Many of our meat dishes are designed for families and will serve 5–7 portions. Preparation times have not been specified as they will differ according to techniques and appliances used. Most ingredients used are easily accessible, however, substitutes can be made where necessary. Where chilli or Scotch bonnet peppers are used, be prepared for fire and heat in the mouth. Removing the seeds will make them less hot. Be sure to wash your hands after handling chilli peppers.

ISBN 978-1-78132-619-0

British Library Cataloguing in Publication Data
A CIP catalogue record for this book is available from the British Library

Page design and typesetting by SilverWood Books
Printed by TJ International on responsibly sourced paper

"Church once weekly made all things well Sunday dinner tummy swell Highly seasoned chicken wings Curry smells and all dem tings."

Taken from 'School Day Memories' by Sherrie Eugene-Hart

Contents

The Carib-Asian Cookery Concept

I'M SO PLEASED TO HAVE been the person that brought *The Carib-Asian Cookery Show* to your television screens back in 2014. I've known and admired Sherrie and her work over many years so for me it was a no brainer to introduce such an original cooking concept to Made In Bristol TV and eventually the entire Made network. After two successive record-breaking series the Carib-Asian concept has swept into our consciousness thanks to this husband-and-wife team Patrick Hart and Sherrie Eugene Hart, who were originally inspired by their mums, Ruth and Rita. What started as a natural blend of fusing food from their families homelands India and Dominica, turned into a gastronomical phenomena as friends and extended family were drawn to the the Hart household to sample their staple diet without an invite.

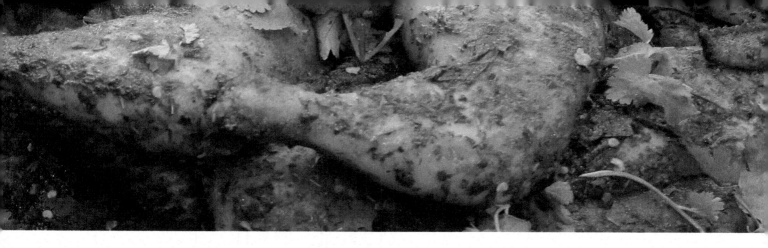

After presenting Carib-Asian cuisine to hundreds of people at food shows Pat was inspired to produce a TV programme which was picked up by me at Made in Bristol TV, transmitting to thousands. What started off as a one-off programme then grew to six and eventually to 14 as other stations in Leeds and Cardiff, Brighton, Tyne and Wear, Birmingham and Liverpool took on the Carib-Asian concept, pushing audience figures into millions. Then came series two, another roller-coaster ride increasing even further both the audience and appetite for all things Carib-Asian.

Award-winning Sherrie, a seasoned TV presenter of 30 years, is no stranger to cookery programmes. At one stage she travelled the Caribbean, looking at the authentic dishes of each island. Patrick, a radio production maverick and station manager of multi award-winning station Bcfm, was compelled to turn his hand to TV production and worked alongside Mike Jenkins of 8th Sense Media to develop the concept and make the *Carib-Asian Cookery Show* happen.

It's not unusual to find Pat and Sherrie on stage working together, presenting award ceremonies and Media / Diversity training for their ethical company, e-com Media, or indeed making TV programmes on real-life subjects, but this duo are rarely seen in the kitchen together. The naturalness of their presentation at home in their own kitchen produced both sparks and spice as they laugh their way through the recipes.

Enjoy your cooking experience and be inspired by this duo and their Carib-Asian recipes! I'm proud to have played a part in exposing this amazing concept to a wider audience.

Chris James, Made TV

About Pat & Sherrie

BRISTOL-BORN SHERRIE EUGENE-HART has enjoyed over 30 years of broadcasting.

She started with HTV Bristol as the sign-language interpreter for deaf viewers and went on to present everything from sport to current affairs, human interest to community interest and children's to cookery. The award winning presenter eventually anchored the nightly flagship news programme *HTV News*.

Sherrie travelled the Caribbean with her production *Sugar and Spice* exploring the authentic dishes of each Island. She also presented the Vegetarian cookery programme *Green Grow the Dishes*. Sherrie admits she honed her culinary skills from her mother Rita, who, together with Sherrie's father Hector, came to Bristol from the idyllic Caribbean Island of Dominica in 1960.

Sherrie continues to produce human interest documentaries and has over the last few years enjoyed writing poetry.

The Carib-Asian concept was born when Sherrie married musician, music producer and broadcaster Patrick, whose parents Ruth and John hail from India.

Patrick Hart has spent most of his life in Bristol, after moving there at the age of 13 from Nottingham.

His culinary skills were also inspired by his mum, who cooked Indian, Italian, Greek and English dishes at home. A successful recording artist and founder of the legendary group Freshblood Crew, he sold hundreds of thousands of records. Patrick used that love of music coupled with his passion for sport to form a multi-million pound youth and media consultancy.

Patrick is currently living his passion as CEO of multi award-winning radio station BCfm, providing 'Culture Change' consultancy services to corporate clients, making and developing new radio and television programme strands and, of course, fulfilling his role as a father as well as being a contributor and speaker for an array of other media organisations.

He's no stranger to fusing occupations and together with Sherrie, alongside their ethical broadcast arm E-Com Media, they're fusing Caribbean and Asian cuisine in their own inimitable style, bringing this brand new concept to our screens and now through the pages of this book.

Welcome

WELCOME TO OUR VERY FIRST *Carib-Asian Cookery Book: Recipes and Rhymes.*

We've loved putting our recipes together, matching them with photos and stories of growing up, together with lyrics from our songs and lines from our poetry.

We've tried and tested them over and over again so that they're just right, and we're sure that you will be able to replicate them and even put your own twist on some.

You'd be forgiven for thinking that Carib-Asian derives from the Carib food tradition born from the Carib Indians, who migrated to the Caribbean in dugout canoes from the Orinoco river. We certainly cannot deny that some of the flavours are not apparent in our dishes. It's a real melting pot of West African Caribbean, Asian and English flavours.

Carib-Asian cooking is not solely a trade name but a brand. In its broadest terms, it's based on the blending of flavours from the Caribbean and Asia, and the bringing together of culinary ideas. It's about sharing cooking concepts as well as flavours but also mixing it up. For example, we will serve ackee and saltfish with paratha and coriander garnish, or add callaloo and sweet potato to a traditional bombay aloo (spinach and potato) dish, or just add some spice and extra ingredients to a traditional shepherd's pie or Italian bolognese.

Apart from the obvious onions garlic and chilli, the flavours in our cooking seem to come from 7 other main ingredients: cardamom, thyme, pimento, garam masala, coriander, curry and all-purpose seasoning. You won't go far wrong if you keep these ingredients in your kitchen.

Just as we enjoy cooking, we hope you do too. We didn't anticipate the sheer joy that came from cooking in the kitchen together whilst making our *Carib-Asian Cookery* shows. So, despite the bickering about spice quantity, portion size and presentation, blending our spices and savouring the flavours were enormously satisfying, especially when shared with family and friends. All our recipes are highly achievable, so don't be afraid to put your own slant on things. There are no strict rules really so just try to enjoy, and even if you don't cook with confidence, be sure to cook with love.

Pat & Sherrie's Tips Before You Get Started

NOT ALL OF US ARE regular book readers so we've tried to keep our book easy to follow for all ages.

We've divided the recipes into categories: Chicken, Red Meat, Fish and Vegetarian. You can make your own adjustments to quantities and some ingredients according to taste. Sherrie will always sprinkle fresh lemon or lime over the chicken before seasoning (she says it cleanses it); however, Pat may not do this and maybe use a rice vinegar or nothing at all.

When marinating meat or fish it's always best to do this overnight as it improves the flavour. Also there is value in seasoning meat and fish dishes with your hands and really getting stuck in. Be sure to wash your hands properly before and after though!

We've numbered each recipe method to make it clearer but we haven't stated the obvious like 'wash your hands first'. Many of the dishes, like dumplings and chapatis, require you to use your hands so you may want to consider keeping nails short and clean.

Don't be afraid to ask other family members how they do things and experiment with your friends. That way you'll get honest feedback so you can always improve your culinary skills. It can also be a great idea to cook with your friends or family and learn together.

Take your time, especially if you're trying something new. It's never good to stress yourself when your guests are arriving in an hour and actually food often tastes much better when prepared earlier.

Get all of your ingredients and utensils ready before starting the cooking process. Chop the onions, garlic, ginger etc and get all of your required spices and other ingredients in front of you, like a painter with their paint pallette, ready to create a masterpiece.

It's useful to use a pestle and mortar (if you can) to grind down your own spice mixes. This brings a uniquely fresh aroma to your dishes and you know exactly what's gone into it.

Now get cooking!

"On the veranda silence is broken by the sound of excitable children all vying to be the loudest. Their cries are diluted by the sound of chickens and goats, harmonising with the existing choir. The chickens have it!"

Taken from 'Caribbean Moments' by Sherrie Eugene-Hart

Chicken

Tip For an extra kick brush with a mixture of honey and hot pepper sauce. Serve with salad. For this dish you can use lamb, beef or fish instead of chicken if you prefer.

IT WAS BITTERLY COLD OUTSIDE and the BBQ in the garden was covered with ice and the breath of winter, yet we were determined to make chicken kebabs. So, after filling the skewers, we started them off in a large frying pan on the hob and finished them off in the oven. Voila. Winter or not, have hob? Will cook! **SERVES 5**

Chicken Kebabs

3 large chicken breasts cubed
2 red peppers
2 green peppers
1 large onion

Chicken seasoning
Coriander chopped finely
Soy sauce
Juice from a lemon

Kebab sticks (soaked in water if wooden)
Oil for frying
Coriander

1   In a bowl, season the chicken with chicken seasoning, coriander and soy sauce.

2   Cut the onions and peppers into cubes and thread the meat and veg alternatively onto the sticks.

3   Set aside for at least an hour to marinade (overnight preferably).

4   Heat a flat pan or griddle with oil and fry kebabs gently for around 4 minutes each side.

5   Finish off in a hot oven for at least 15 minutes at gas mark 5.

WHEN YOU FANCY A CURRY it can actually be easier to make one at home rather than reach for the phone, especially on a Friday or Saturday night when your local can take up to an hour to deliver. I can make this in less than an hour. **SERVES 4 GENEROUS PORTIONS**

Pat's Quick Chicken Curry

3 chicken breasts cubed
1 large onion finely chopped
1 thumb size of ginger finely chopped
4 garlic cloves finely chopped

1 chilli (optional)
1 tin of chopped tomatoes
Half bottle of curry paste ?
Generous splash of rice vinegar
2 tbs chicken seasoning

2 tbs curry powder (Mild)
Juice from 1 lemon
Olive oil (4- 6 tbs)

1   Wash the chicken with the juice from a lemon.

2   Season with 1 tbs curry powder and 1 tbs chicken seasoning (save the rest for later). Set aside.

3   In a hot pan fry the the onion, ginger, garlic and chilli together with the remaining curry powder and chicken seasoning with 3 tablespoons of olive oil and cook through.

4   Add the tin of tomatoes, rice vinegar and the curry paste.

5   Finally add the chicken and the whole chilli with the rest of the olive oil and simmer for 45 minutes. Stir from time to time and add a little water if it starts to stick.

6   Garnish with coriander.

 Tip You could use chicken on the bone chopped into bite-sized pieces (it will take around 15 minutes longer). Serve with rice or chapati and a fresh salad.

CARIB-ASIAN FRIED CHICKEN CAN be served as part of a large buffet, a meal at home, or even for a packed lunch. Either way you're going to want to use your fingers and lick them afterwards. This scrumptious dish is packed with Carib-Asian flavours and is quite addictive. Be warned! **SERVES 5**

Carib-Asian Fried Chicken

5 large chicken pieces (skin on)
1 tbs of chicken seasoning
1 tbs of curry powder
1 tbs garam masala powder
1 star anise

Half tsp of crushed dry
cardamom seeds
Half tsp of crushed cloves
1 onion chopped chunky
4 cloves garlic chopped

1 green chilli whole
Handful of coriander
1 lemon

1 Squeeze the lemon over the chicken.

2 Smother the chicken with all the dry seasonings, mix and leave to marinade in the fridge for a few hours or overnight.

3 Heat a large frying pan. Add oil and all the crushed ingredients.

4 After a few minutes add the onion, garlic, chilli pepper, star anise and coriander. Fry until soft, and remove from the pan.

5 Heat more oil and fry the chicken until golden on both sides and nearly cooked inside. This should take about 10 minutes on each side.

6 Re-introduce the onion mixture and continue to fry.

7 After about 30 minutes and when both sides are brown, your Carib-Asian chicken will be ready.

 Feel free to cut the chicken portions before cooking if it helps. Serve with fresh onion and tomatoes.

Tip This works just as well with larger chicken pieces. Serve with pumpkin rice and chapati.

IF YOU LIKE CHICKEN AND you like orange, you'll love this unusual combination! **SERVES 5**

Sticky Orange Chicken

1lb chicken pieces (on the bone optional)
Juice from 5 large oranges
1 onion chopped
1 red sweet pepper

1 green chilli pepper
Generous sprigs of thyme
1 cinnamon stick
1tbs chicken seasoning
1tbs garam masala

2 tbsp of honey
Half a bunch of coriander
Splash of soy sauce
1 maggi cube
1 lemon

1 Season the chicken. Start by squeezing the juice from the lemon and from 1 orange onto it.

2 Smother with chicken seasoning, garam masala, half of the chopped coriander and a splash of soy sauce.

3 Set aside and allow to marinade for at least 30 minutes.

4 Heat the onions in hot oil, together with the sweet red pepper, chilli pepper, thyme, cinnamon stick and maggi cube.

5 After a couple minutes when it's started to sizzle, add half the juice from the oranges and the honey.

6 Add the chicken to the sauce and cook rapidly for about 3 minutes. If it starts to stick, add the rest of the orange juice, put a lid on and turn the heat right down until it is cooked.

7 Remove the cinnamon stick and thyme stalks, and garnish with coriander.

WE MADE SPICEY CHICKEN WINGS on our pilot tv programme for the *Carib-Asian Cookery* show. This is a cheap and cheerful dish which looks good as a centre piece. We've included mango to zing it up even more. Now it's become a firm favourite with so many of our viewers. **SERVES 5**

Mango Chicken Wings

15 chicken wings sprinkled in lemon water
1 large firm mango chopped (keep seed for stock)
1 large onion chopped
1 yellow pepper chopped

5 garlic cloves chopped
3 bay leaves
Fresh thyme
3 tbs mango chutney
Coriander to garnish
2 tbs of garam masala

2 tbs of chicken masala seasoning
1 tbs of all-purpose seasoning
1 lemon for washing the chicken
Pre-cooked rice as a bed for the chicken

1 Clean the chicken with water and the juice from a lemon.

2 Season with chicken seasoning, garam masala and all-purpose seasoning. Mix thoroughly, using your hands preferably.

3 Heat oil in frying pan and sweat the chicken. Add half cup of water and cover for 10 minutes or until boiling.

4 Remove from the pan and continue to cook in the oven on gas mark 6. Leave to brown for 45 minutes, turning occasionally. There should be a small amount of chicken stock left in the pan (keep this).

5 While the chicken is in the oven, add the onions, garlic, pepper thyme and bay leaves to the stock left in the pan. Add the remaining seasonings and a half glass of water to loosen.

6 Chop half the mango into cubes and add to the mixture, scraping as much mango as you can from the skin. Save the other half of the mango for garnish. Add the mango pip in the stock mixture. Remove it later. Continue to fry until the juice looks like a dry curry.

7   If the chicken in the oven has produced more juice, then pour it into the onion mixture, sizzle it through, add three tbs mango chutney and turn off the heat (add a little water to loosen if you have to). Remove the mango seed and discard.

8   Place your cooked wings on a serving dish and spoon the onion mixture over the chicken evenly.

9   Garnish with the remainder of mango and fresh coriander and serve hot. Delicious!

THE REDNESS OF THE CHICKEN gives this dish its Tandoori title, not the fact that it has been cooked in a Tandoor oven, because it hasn't. It's brilliant cooked on a BBQ or in the conventional oven. Serve with rice and peas and a nice slaw. **SERVES 6**

Tandoori Chicken Caribbean Style

12 chicken pieces soaked in lemon water
1 lemon
Half a jar of tandoori paste

I large tub of natural yoghurt
½ tsp clove powder
½ tsp cinnamon powder
2 tbs of chicken seasoning

1 tbs all-purpose seasoning
1 tbs black pepper
Bunch of coriander divided into two

1 Scar the lemon-soaked chicken with a sharp knife to allow the seasoning to infuse.

2 Smother with all-purpose seasoning and chicken seasoning. Set aside.

3 Mix the tandoori paste, black pepper, clove powder, cinnamon powder and natural yoghurt together with half the coriander and smother over the chicken. Leave to marinade for at least 2 hours. Overnight is better.

4 Decant into a baking pan and place in a hot oven, gas mark 5 for 2 hours, turning occasionally.

5 If there is any yogurt left, smother it over the chicken after an hour.

6 When cooked sprinkle with coriander and serve hot or cold.

 Tip Serving with rice and peas gives this dish a nice fusion twist (see vegetarian and vegan section).

WE LIKE WET FOOD! ANYTHING with rice requires for us 'wet food'. It's not for everyone, but we've been very versatile in this book, and Brown Stew Chicken is a wet food favourite. This is the way we do it! **SERVES 8**

Carib-Asian Brown Stew Chicken

2lb chicken pieces
1 tbs chicken seasoning
1 tbs curry powder
1 tbs garam masala powder
Dry crushed ingredients with
pestle and mortar

Half tsp crushed cloves
Half tsp pimento seeds
1 tsp crushed allspice
1 diced onion
4 cloves garlic chopped
Handful of coriander

Bunch of fresh thyme
1 whole Scotch bonnet
1 lemon
Splash of gravy browning
1 maggi cube

1   Squeeze the lemon over the chicken. Smother the chicken with all the dry seasonings and leave to marinade in the fridge for a few hours or overnight.

2   In a large frying pan heat the oil and add the dry crushed ingredients. Use a pestle and mortar to crush if you have one – otherwise use ready ground spices.

3   After a few minutes add the onion, garlic, coriander and thyme.

4   Fry until soft, then add the chicken and cook over a medium heat.

5   Add half a cup of water and cover. After about 30 minutes and when both sides are brown, add your gravy browning, maggi cube and Scotch bonnet. Simmer until ready (about 15 minutes).

 Tip Do not stir vigorously. It will break up the chicken pieces. The Scotch bonnet pepper is there for decoration and subtle flavour. Do not break the skin unless you want the hot pepper flavour to evade the dish. Serve with rice and peas or Basmati rice and cabbage Jolfry.

THERE'S SOMETHING HUGELY SATISFYING ABOUT eating with your fingers, using roti or naan bread to sap up the sauce is a must. Here's a dish where you can do just that. **SERVES 6**

Chicken with Roti and Chilli Plum Sauce

2lb chicken pieces chopped into bite-size pieces
1 large onion chopped
4 cloves garlic chopped
1 tbs chicken masala

2 chilli peppers
1 tsp pimento seeds
5 small cloves
3 bay leaves
Half bunch coriander

1 tsp mustard seeds
4/6 cardamom seeds
Splash of oil
6 ready bought roti
Juice from a lemon

Method for chicken

1   Squeeze lemon over the chicken.

2   Season it with the chicken masala powder.

3   Using a pestle and mortar grind the chilli peppers, pimento seeds, cloves, mustard seeds ,cardamom pods, garlic cloves, bay leaves, coriander leaves and a little oil.

4   Smother your paste over the chicken. Use your hands if you prefer. Cover and set aside to marinade.

For the chilli plum sauce

Half jar plum jam (seedless)
5 dried plums roughly chopped
(prunes work just as well)
1 red onion finely chopped

Thumb size of ginger chopped
4 red chillies (keep seeds in for
extra hotness)
Half a mug of malt vinegar

1 tsp mustard seeds
Pinch of salt

Method for plum sauce

1   Fry the chillies, onion and ginger until soft.

2   Add the plums or prunes and mustard seeds
    and stir.

3   Then add plum jam and vinegar and stir until
    the liquid reduces to a sauce like consistency.
    Stir.

4   Add a pinch of salt and set aside. When cooled
    your sauce is ready.

To cook your chicken

1   By now your chicken would have been nicely
    marinaded. In a hot pan with a splash of oil,
    fry your seasoned chicken, turning
    occasionally until all sides are brown.

2   Add your onions and mix through.

3   Warm your roti.

4   To serve individually, spoon a portion of
    chicken on a bed of roti, dot some plum sauce
    around and garnish with coriander leaves.

 Tip   Use just 1 fresh chilli or de seed them if you prefer a less hot dish. Also use naan
bread or chapati as an alternative to roti.

COCONUT SAUCE IS AN ASIAN favourite. This dish is not as mild as Korma and not as hot as a Madras. Like so many of our recipes it's packed with flavour and intrigue and is a Carib-Asian favourite and delight. **SERVES 6**

Coconut and Coriander Chicken

2lb chicken pieces
1 tin coconut milk
1 bunch coriander chopped
1 onion finely chopped
5 cloves of garlic finely chopped

1 star anise
2 tbs chicken masala
1 tsp black pepper
2 tbs garam masala
Cinnamon stick

1 lemon
Splash of oil
Coconut shavings (optional)

1 Smother the chicken with the lemon juice.

2 Season with 1 tbs chicken seasoning, 1 tbs garam masala, ½ tsp black pepper, and half a bunch of chopped coriander.

3 Mix with your hands if you can handle it. Set aside.

4 Heat the oil in a large pan.

5 Fry the onion, garlic, star anise and coriander together (save a little coriander for the garnish at the end).

6 Add the remaining dry seasonings and stir.

7 Add the coconut milk to the mixture and then include the chicken. Make sure the coconut mixture is covering the chicken (if not add a little water).

8 Cover and leave to cook for about 40 minutes on medium to low heat. Check and stir occasionally.

9 Before serving sprinkle with coriander leaves and coconut shavings (optional). Serve with rice or naan bread.

TAKE A HANDFUL OF YOUR favourite veg and spice and add your favourite meat or fish and you've got yourself a culinary carnival. We've used a sumptuous combination of fresh veg and chicken. We cooked this at the London Produce Show in front of 'serious foodies' and the party started! **SERVES 8**

Carib-Asian Jolfry Wrap with Jerk Infused Chicken

4 chicken fillets cubed
2 sweet potato cooked
1 plantain sliced and fried
1 aubergine
Fist full of calalo
1 red capsicum pepper
1 green chilli pepper

1/4 white cabbage thinly chopped
1/4 red cabbage thinly chopped
4 garlic cloves
1 small onion
8 roti
3 crushed cardamoms
½ tsp black pepper

1 tbs jerk seasoning paste
or powder
1tbs turmeric
Fresh coriander leaves for
garnish
A few sprigs of fresh thyme
8 spoons of mango chutney

1 Season the cubed chicken with half of all the dry seasoning powders and mix through thoroughly and set aside.

2 In a large pan with a splash of oil, fry the onions, garlic, aubergine, chilli and capsicum pepper. Add the red and white cabbage, calaloo and thyme.

3 Sprinkle on the rest of the dry seasonings and give a good stir. Add a little more oil if you need to.

4 Remove from the pan and set aside.

5 In the same pan, heat some oil and fry the chicken until golden brown. Add the fried plantain.

6 On a warm roti spread on a thin layer of mango chutney and spoon on the filling.

7 Sprinkle with chopped Coriander and serve immediately.

 You can use chapati or even naan bread with this dish. Make sure any root vegetables like sweet potatoes or yams are cooked through first to soften them. TOP TIP: Use fish instead of chicken if you like.

IF YOU'VE GOT A BIT of time on your hands make the most of this show stopper. It's great for a dinner party, impressive on the plate, but more than that it's great on the pallet. SERVES 4–8

Carib-Asian Stuffed Chicken Breast

4 chicken breasts 1 tbs chicken seasoning	1tbs paprika 1 tsp cumin powder	Juice from a lemon

For the stuffing

1 onion chopped 2 spring onions chopped 3 garlic cloves	1 punnet of mushrooms 1 tbs all purpose seasoning Handful of coriander	Sprigs of thyme

1 Smother the chicken with lemon juice.

2 Slice halfway open.

3 Season with chicken seasoning and paprika and cumin.

4 Using a liquidiser mince the mushrooms, onion, spring onion, garlic, coriander and thyme.

5 Stuff the chicken breasts and use a cocktail stick to close them.

6 In a hot pan with a splash of oil, gently brown the breasts on each side and finish off in the oven for about 35–40 minutes.

7 When ready carefully slice in two and arrange on a plate serve with a fresh salad and rice.

Tip Feel free to stuff with seasoned rice or other veg of your choice.

"Our mum is phenomenal. She homes a deep intelligence that I could only dream of. She's wonderful, beautiful. Her beauty was then, is now, and forever will be inside and out. She's funny, her humour stretching across the miles. Her nuance and expressions cause the smiles."

Taken from 'Our mum is phenomenal' by Sherrie Eugene-Hart

I FIRST VISITED DOMINICA WITH my mum when I was seventeen. Being the baby of the family, I was last of the siblings to go there after Paula and Judy. My other older sisters Corinne, Dagma Lena and Gean were all born in Dominica, and I couldn't wait to see where they had grown up. The image I remember from the tiny plane when making the descent onto the beautiful island was the coconut trees lining the beach. I was also taken back by the forests of banana trees and the overall lushness of the nature island. When I arrived at my grandmother's house in Mahaut the first thing that hit me was the aroma of richly seasoned meat bubbling in the pot, as Mama presented me with coconut milk served in its own shell and husk. In the afternoon I took a bus to the next village in Massacre where Aunty Victoria cooked a huge 'bomb' of 'one pot hold all'. Boy, that was so nice and boy, I was so home.

"My folks came over here to start a new life. What
they encountered was
hardship & strife
Taking work they were
overqualified. But their spirit
never died,
I'm livin' proud that the vision
I posses is born from love
nothing more nothing less,
To the truth that is shining
through, my mum & dad
this is for you."

Taken from 'Days Gone By' – Freshblood Crew – *The Definitive Freshblood Collection* – Freshblood Records 2015

I'M LUCKY ENOUGH TO HAVE had the blessing of my mum Ruth in my life until November 2009. She really was the centre of our family and to be honest the centre of my world. From a really young age, whilst my three brothers were at the park playing football I'd often be at home with Mum, thinking I was looking after her as she was often in and out of hospital. Really she was looking after me as I watched her cook and prepare food often from fairly bare cupboards. The menu was varied; English, Greek, Italian and Asian cuisine were regularly fused in what Mum would call her 'concoctions'. It wasn't until my later years that I realised how much of Mum's culinary skills had soaked in and also how, like her, I loved to look after the people around me. What better way to look after someone then cook for them?

"We didn't have a pestle and mortar in our house; we didn't need one. You see, mum used a milk bottle to mash garlic cloves or peppercorns. That same milk bottle doubled as a rolling pin too. To me that was normal. Even though I've picked up so much from Mum, today she uses a pestle and mortar so that's one thing she's got from me. That's what I call a throwback from history."

Red Meat

EVERYBODY LOVES A GOOD STEW in the winter. Mum used to make a variation of this with homegrown carrots and pumpkin. My inspiration for this dish comes directly from Mum in the kitchen and Dad at the allotment at winter time. SERVES 5–7

Chilli Lamb and Sweet Potato Stew

2lb lamb diced (with bone optional)
3 large carrots and diced
2 large sweet potatoes diced
1 yellow yam diced
1 large onion diced

5 cloves of garlic
2 red chillies diced
3 tbs of lamb seasoning
2 tbs garam masala
1 tbs all-purpose seasoning
½ tsp black pepper

½ caraway seeds
4 bay leaves
Knob of butter
1 pint lamb stock from a cube or
2 maggi cubes

For the dumplings

3 cups of self raising flour
½ tsp dried thyme
Pinch of salt

1   Season the lamb with all the dry seasonings and mix in thoroughly.

2   Fry the onions, garlic, chilli, carrots, sweet potato and yam. After a few minutes and over medium heat add the seasoned lamb and sweat until the lamb starts to stick to the pan.

3   Add the stock and cover. Cook for an hour over low heat, stirring occasionally.

4   The lamb should be tender and cooking in its stock. Have a taste and add a maggi cube or two if it needs it and a thickening agent if you want to. Simmer.

5   Quickly make your dumplings by mixing the flour, water, thyme and a pinch of salt together. Use your hands and form the dough into circles.

6   Pour your meat mixture into a casserole dish
    and drop the dumplings on top until the stew is
    covered. Don't worry if the stock is overflowing.

7   Put in the oven on a medium heat and cook for
    a further 35–45 minutes or until the meat is
    tender and the gravy bubbling over.

8   Garnish with coriander and fresh chopped
    chilli and serve piping hot. Lovely!

IT'S WINTER, IT'S COLD AND we've just got home from school. Mum is home and cooking dinner. I open the door and the warmth of the kitchen and the waft of spicy mince hits me instantly. It's at this point I know we're in for a hearty meal. This is no ordinary spag bol. The principals are the same but the spice blend is sublime. SERVES 5

Carib-Asian Spag Bol

2lb lamb mince / 1kg 900g
1 large chopped onion
1 chopped Scotch bonnet or chilli pepper (remove seeds to reduce heat)
1 tin tomatoes

Large squirt tomato puree
4 chopped garlic cloves
1 tsp thyme
1 tsp black pepper
1 tbs all-purpose seasoning
1 tbs curry powder

DRY seasoning

Splash of Lea & Perrins sauce
Dash of oil
Cooked spaghetti or other pasta like twists or shells

1   Season mince with half of the chopped onion, half of the Scotch bonnet and half of the garlic.

2   Season with half of all the dry seasonings and mix with your hands. Set aside.

3   Heat the oil in a pan. Fry the other half of the onion, the remaining garlic, thyme and Scotch bonnet pepper until well sweated.

4   Add the mince and fry for 10 minutes. Add a cup full of water together with the tomato puree and cook through for at least 30 minutes. Stir occasionally.

5   Finally add the tin tomatoes and cook for at least 10 minutes then add a splash of Lea & Perrins sauce before serving with spaghetti.

> **Tip** Use pasta twists or other pasta if you prefer and sprinkle with a mild cheddar cheese.

A REAL TWIST ON A British classic. Empty bellies and hungry eyes witness a wholesome dish coming out of the oven in slow motion, dribbling with meat juices and melted cheese as it lands on the table piping hot. Life is good! **SERVES 5**

Carib-Asian Shepherd's Pie

2lb mince meat (beef or lamb)
2 carrots finely chopped
2 celery sticks finely chopped
1 onion chopped
4 cloves garlic chopped

1 chilli pepper (seeded optional)
1 tbs all-purpose seasoning
1 tbs paprika
1 tsp cumin powder
1 tsp curry powder

1 tsp black pepper
1 tin tomatoes
Splash of oil
Splash of soy sauce

For the topping

4 large potatoes cooked and mashed
1 onion sliced into rings

1 aubergine sliced and lightly fried
Cheese to sprinkle on top

2 large sweet potatoes cooked and mashed

1 Season the mince with the all-purpose, paprika, cumin, curry and black pepper powder. Mix with your fingers – it's therapeutic and more fun! Set aside for at least half hour.

2 Heat a pan with a splash of oil. Fry the onions, chilli, garlic, carrot and celery.

3 Add the mince meat and fry for 10 minutes or until partly cooked through.

4 Add the tinned tomatoes and a splash of soy sauce. Leave to simmer for a further 35–40 minutes. Add a little water if it starts to dry.

5 When the meat is cooked, pour into a baking dish. Smooth the potato over the top, followed by a layer of sliced cooked aubergine, a layer of onion rings and a sprinkling of cheese.

6 Bake in the oven for 30 minutes or until the top is golden brown. Serve hot. Delicious!

Tip Add sliced tomatoes together with the aubergines. Serve with a nice crunchy salad.

IN OUR HOUSE, SOUP WAS never soup unless it was thick and filled with veg and meat. So here's our Carib-Asian version of Saturday Soup. When you taste this, you'll want it every day. Give yourself at least 2 ½ to 3 hours cooking time. **SERVES 6 GENEROUS PORTIONS**

Carib-Asian Everyday Soup

2lb lamb back chopped
3 tbs achar gosht seasoning powder (masala if you can't find any)
3 green bananas
4 edos cubed (type of yam)
4 large potatoes cubed
1 large onion chopped
½ pumpkin cubed

1 capsicum red pepper chopped
1 seeded Scotch bonnet
1 packet pumpkin soup
4 garlic cloves chopped
5 twigs of thyme
3 bay leaves
1 tsp black pepper
1 tsp pimento seeds
1 tsp black mustard seeds

1 tsp turmeric
1 tbs all purpose seasoning
2 maggi cubes,
Use any root vegetables of choice like dasheen
2 cups of plain flour
½ cup of water for little dumplings
Bunch of calaloo or spinach

1 Season the meat using achar gosht powder and mix with your hands.

2 Ideally, leave overnight. If not give it a few hours or enough time to marinade.

3 In the meantime, using a large soup pot, fry your onions, red pepper, Scotch bonnet and garlic.

4 Add the thyme, bay leaves, pimento seeds and mustard seeds. Stir and loosen with a little water.

5 Add the dry seasonings, black pepper, all-purpose seasoning and turmeric to the mixture.

6 Now add the meat, mix and sweat. After 5 minutes or so add 2 litres of stock or water and leave to boil. Increase the heat.

7 Remove any froth from the stock that may appear from the meat during the boiling process.

8 After an hour or so add the green banana, potatoes, pumpkin and any vegetables of your choice.

9   Add another 2 litres of stock or water and boil for a further hour.

10 When the meat is tender, add the packet soup, maggi cubes and calaloo or spinach and simmer for a further 30 minutes.

11 Finally make little dumplings by mixing flour and water and a pinch of salt. Shape little round dumplings and drop them into the soup together with finely chopped coriander. In 5 minutes your soup will be ready. It should be rich and wholesome.

YOU KNOW THE FEELING YOU get when eating a doughnut and you get to the jam? Well it's the same feeling you get when eating these potato cakes. Make sure you pack it with spice mince and you won't be disappointed.

Spice Mince Potato Cakes

6 large potatoes mashed with
a knob of butter and a little milk
1lb minced lamb meat
1 large onion finely chopped
1 chilli pepper finely chopped

3 garlic cloves finely chopped
Handful of coriander
For the pestle and mortar
3/4 cardamom seeds
2 cloves

5/6 pimento seeds
1 star anise
2 eggs whipped
Breadcrumbs
Oil for frying

1 Using a pestle and mortar, crush your cardamoms, cloves, pimento seeds and star anise.

2 Fry the crushed spices in hot oil.

3 Add onion, garlic coriander and all-purpose seasoning.

4 Add your mince to the spices and cook through for at least 10 minutes. Have a taste and add more seasoning if you need to. Set aside.

5 Season the mashed potato with lamb seasoning and mix through thoroughly.

6 This bit will be messy but enjoy it nevertheless. Make a ball shape with the mash, make a hole and put a generous spoonful of mince inside. Close it up and repeat the process until the end.

7 Coat the cakes in egg wash and then breadcrumbs.

8 Shallow fry the cakes until golden brown. Finish off in the oven if you want to.

 Use homemade breadcrumbs if you prefer. Also you could use minced chicken instead of lamb. Serve with a crunchy salad and a chilli sauce.

HERE'S A TWIST ON ROAST lamb. If you like your lamb like we do, try this awesome fusion dish. It's a perfect Sunday dinner dish that promises to be a talking point for ages. SERVES 6–8

Masala Lamb

I large lamb leg
1 tbs lamb seasoning
1 tbs garam masala
1 tbs curry powder
Bunch of fresh rosemary

Bunch of Coriander (save a little for garnish)
5 garlic cloves crushed
Large onion chopped
4 chillis red or green whole

Splash of seasoning sauce or light soy sauce
Splash of olive oil

1 Wash the lamb and pierce it. Press garlic deep into the slits.

2 Season with your lamb seasoning, garam masala and curry powder. Massage the seasoning into the lamb. Rub in well. Ideally, leave to marinade overnight or for an hour or so at least.

3 Place in a roasting tin together with your onions, chillies, coriander, any remaining garlic and rosemary.

4 Splash with your seasoning sauce, olive oil and half a cup of water.

5 Cover with foil and put in the oven on the middle shelf for at least 1 ½ to 2 hours on gas mark 5.

6 After an hour or so remove the foil turn the lamb and continue to cook until brown and tender. Garnish with coriander leaves. Delicious with spicy roasters, rice and peas.

 Tip   Use the lamb bone for soup or stock.

58

INDIA IS SEASONING COOKED POTATOES with garam masala, and smothering with chopped coriander and olive oil. Cook in the oven until crispy and golden.

"As a boy they told me not
to feel, to front it out so
                    hurt would heal,
As a youth they said it was
     weak to care,
no tears or emotion
           just a hardened stare,
As a man I knew it would
           not be long,
before my child was born
           and the cold was gone,
As a father now I can watch
                    her grow
and my life is love
that i'm so proud to show."

'A verse for India' by Patrick Hart

AT HOME THESE MORSELS OF sublimeness came in all shapes and sizes. Mum didn't mind how they looked, it was the taste that mattered. The pastry melted in your mouth and the filling was seasoned to perfection. Somehow my friends always managed to be at my house at the right time and you could eat these hot or cold!

Puff Patties

2lb minced lamb or beef
1 large onion diced
4 garlic cloves diced

1 thumb size of ginger
½ tsp cumin seeds
1 tbs mild curry powder

Bunch of coriander chopped
Two rolls of puff pastry

1 Season the mince with the onion, garlic, ginger, curry powder, cumin powder and coriander.

2 Work it through with your hands.

3 Fry the mixture for about 10 minutes and then allow it to cool.

4 Roll out pastry and cut into squares.

5 Spoon the cooled mince into the squares big enough to wrap the pastry into parcels.

6 Use a fork to press the parcels together sealed with milk or egg wash.

7 Brush the patties with egg wash, place on baking tray and bake in a hot oven for 25 minutes or until golden brown.

 Tip Sprinkle a good amount of flour in the baking tray before adding the patties to prevent sticking.

THIS WAS A FIRM FAVOURITE in our house. No sooner had they come out the oven, they were snapped up if Mum didn't fight us off with a tea towel first! These cutlets became a bit of a signature dish for Mum, and my friends would often come round when they knew they were on the menu. I wasn't sharing my last cutlet with anyone, let alone my brothers!

Lamb Cutlets

2lb minced lamb or beef
1 large onion diced
4 garlic cloves diced
1 thumb size of ginger diced

1 tbs mild curry powder
1 tbs garam masala
1 tbs lamb seasoning
Bunch of coriander chopped

Half a cup of breadcrumbs
1 egg

1   Season the mince with the diced onion, garlic, ginger, coriander, breadcrumbs, garam masala, curry powder, lamb seasoning and the egg, and mix through with your hands.

2   Shape the cutlets into small oval burger shapes and place on a greased baking tray.

3   Cook in a hot oven for 30 minutes.

Tip Feel free to fry the cutlets instead of cooking them in the oven. Serve with naan or pita bread, salad and raita.

WHETHER YOU COOK THEM INSIDE on the hob, in the oven, or outside on the BBQ, these food filled sticks look pretty impressive. We cooked king prawn kebabs for our Christmas show which was filmed live! **SERVES 5**

Carib-Asian Lamb Kebabs

1lb lamb cubed
1 red pepper cubed
2 green peppers cubed
1 large onion cubed

1 tbs lamb masala
Bunch coriander chopped finely
Two sprigs chopped rosemary
Splash of soy sauce

Kebab sticks (soaked in water if wooden)
Juice from a lemon
Oil for frying

1   In a bowl, season the lamb with the lamb masala, coriander rosemary and soy sauce.

2   Cut the onions and peppers into cubes and thread the meat and veg alternatively onto the sticks.

3   Set aside for at least an hour to marinade (overnight preferably).

4   Heat a flat pan or griddle with oil and fry kebabs gently for around 4 minutes each side.

5   Finish off in a hot oven for at least 30 minutes at gas mark 5.

 Tip When cooked, brush with a mixture of honey and hot pepper sauce for an extra kick. Serve with salad wrapped in roti. King prawns on the shell are awesome on a skewer. Sprinkle with soy sauce before they go in the oven.

My Caribbean Discovery

GROWING UP AS AN "ANGLO-Indian" in Nottingham and then Bristol meant living a fairly sheltered life and, though we had a happy and fulfilling childhood, our school life and neighbourhoods left us without the experience of growing up in a truly diverse environment. Fast forward to my early 20s when I was managing a reggae artist called Dan Ratchet as part of a group called Freshblood Crew. We were based in Bristol but had a gig at the Podium Banqueting suite in Vauxhall, London, where Dan was performing alongside Janet Kay and boxing champ Lloyd Honeyghan. It was a big gig for us, hosted by Tony Williams from Radio London. We'd travelled all day and it was well into the evening when a lady asked us if we wanted to eat. There were a couple of English lads with us too and we would have eaten anything! That was my first experience of curry goat, and it was like meeting a new friend that I knew would be with me for the rest of my life. The heat and spice and the soft, succulent goat meat on the bone mixed with rice and peas was just what I needed – what we all needed in fact. I had three plates and all I could think about on the way home at 4am was where I was going to get food like that again.

"Palm trees sprouting out
of luscious fertile soil.
Banana branches
stretching out like
propellers.
Passion fruit bushes
generous with its
scrumptious donations,
And Mango trees
drooping with
juice ready circles
of sweetness."

Taken from 'Caribbean Moments' by Sherrie Eugene-Hart

WHETHER IT BE A WEDDING, or funeral, christening, or birthday party, if celebrated properly according to many Caribbean people, Curry Goat will be on the menu! If not something is seriously wrong. Be suspicious of people who call it Goat Curry. It's not. It's definitely Curry Goat, and a signature dish on many of the Caribbean Islands. Each Island will have their slant on the recipe and each household too, so this is our Carib-Asian take on Curry Goat. SERVES 6–8 GOOD PORTIONS

Carib-Asian Curry Goat

2lb goat meat chopped into bite-sized pieces (with bone)
3 scallion or spring onion chopped
1 onion chopped
6 garlic cloves chopped

2 bay leaves
5 sticks of fresh thyme
1 large potato
1 scotch bonnet pepper
Juice from 1 lime
1 tsp black pepper

3 tbs curry powder
2 tbs allspice or pimento seeds crushed (it's the same thing)
1 tbs garam masala
1 tbs brown sugar
Splash of vegetable oil

1   After washing your meat, sprinkle with lime juice ready for seasoning.

2   Apply all your dry seasonings onto the meat and mix well with your hands.

3   Add your spring onions, onions, garlic, Scotch bonnet and mix with your hands.

4   Leave to marinate overnight or at least for 3 hours.

5   In a large pot, heat your oil and start to brown off the meat. This should take about 3–4 minutes.

6   Cover the meat with hot water. Make sure all the meat is submerged.

7   Add your bay leaves, thyme. Cover and cook for 1 ½ hours stirring every half hour and adding more water as it reduces.

8   Then add your potatoes. (You may need extra dry
    seasoning. This is where you add it. For added
    flavour seasoning salt or everyday seasoning).

9   Cook for a further half hour until the potatoes
    start to mash, and the meat is completely
    tender.

10 Finally stir in the brown sugar and cook for
    a further 10 minutes.

 Use mutton or beef if you prefer. Lamb however will require less cooking time.
Serve with Rice and Peas. (See vegetarian and vegan section).

LIVER WAS A COMMON DISH in both of our households, both of us enjoyed onion gravy, onions and mash with it. We've decided to take it a step further and introduce pumpkin.

Liver in Pumpkin Parcels

1 lb lambs liver
1 tbs liver seasoning (if you can find it) OR 1 tsp everyday seasoning
½ tsp cumin powder

½ tsp curry powder
1 onion chopped
Splash of oil
1 large chopped tomato for garnish

Plain flour to coat liver
1 medium size pumpkin halved and seeded
Splash of olive oil
Sprinkle of onion salt

Method for the Pumpkin

1 Sprinkle onion salt and olive oil in the pumpkin shells. Cover with foil and bake in a hot oven until soft. This will take about an hour and half. Check after an hour.

Method for the Liver

1 Slice the liver into slithers. Season with all the seasonings and mix with a spoon. Coat with flour until all the liver is covered. Set aside.

2 Fry the onions in hot oil and add the liver. Cook for at least 5 minutes on each side and set aside.

3 After the pumpkin has been baking for at least an hour, spoon the liver into the pumpkin shells and put back into the oven, and cover with foil for a further 30 minutes.

 Serve with mash potato and a nice thick gravy.

"I'm no stranger to cooking in front of the camera but I've come to realise that the *Carib-Asian Cookery* show is like nothing I've ever experienced. Cooking in your own kitchen is one thing; cooking with your husband is quite another! Although we love the Carib-Asian experience, we seldom agree on dishes – let alone the recipe – but are always pleasantly surprised by the results. But when we decided on the ingredients for the Carib-Asian flavour there was no argument; it was simple. Three typical Asian spices, three typical Caribbean spices and three staples. Bingo! Roll cameras."

Going Back, Looking Forward

MY CHOSEN CAREER PATH WAS not shaped by drama school or a media course but a willingness to learn and encouragement from my family. My mum taught me to cook, my sister judy taught me to sign and being in the right place at the right time gave me my first break in TV.

I do believe it's not where you come from or how much money you have but the influences you have in your life and belief in yourself that nurtures success and helps to shape your path. I used to feel confident when others said I could do it. Now I just get on and do things without waiting for the confirmation.

"They brought us up strict
with lots of love
The moment we spoke
a book they would shove
In front of our faces
knowing the need
To recognise letters in order
to read.
Early school fascinating,
fun games and play.
Lunch was the best
shepherd's pie carrots
and egg curry
soon realised lunch was the
least of my worry."

Taken from 'School Day Memories' by Sherrie Eugene-Hart

The Lads – Blood May Be Thicker than Water but You Must Have Water to Live!

I'VE ALWAYS HAD THE SAME group of people around me throughout most of my life. As part of a family of six there were, of course, my brothers, but anyone from a large family will know that when the time comes you need to go out and "fly the nest" just to prove you can survive without that support. Being the person that I am, though, I grew a new support network with a group of lads that are now a very important part of my family and who have seen me through some tough times. It's an essential part of our well-being to know that we have people there for us no matter what happens, offering that unconditional love and support. Of course, food has always played an important part in our lives and those relationships too. Being on the road with the Freshblood Crew and touring around the world meant some amazing culinary experiences that still influence our eating habits back home. Spice, curry, chicken and rice are never far away and, of course, alongside the love of my mum Ruth and dad John, those foods a staple at home too.

"It's impossible to live without purpose,
you're going under if you think that
life's worthless, I'm telling you
because I know a better way,
you've got to strive to make
a purpose for your day.
It's not impossible to give if it's life
that you really want to live,
You only get what you put in and
people's love is what you win.
It's kind of difficult to say,
but there is another way
All you have to do is pray and let
your God out to play.
Every morning I wake up looking
to a brighter day
Always chasing what I want,
I couldn't see it your way."

Taken from 'Every Morning' – Freshblood Crew – *The Definitive Freshblood Collection* – Freshblood Records

FISH AND SEAFOOD RESONATE STRONGLY both in the Caribbean and Asia. I remember Mum buying fish from Toveys fishmonger in Bristol. I'm sure Mr Tovey was happy to gut the fish, but somehow Mum always came home with a full belly of fish to be gutted in our backyard. How things change! 40 years later I still shop at Toveys but always take advantage of the offer of gutting! Mum would also leave the heads on always. To this day fish heads do not offend me. In fact, even when I cut them off, I use them for boiling to make stock. Just add a few sprigs of thyme, a bay leaf, onion, garlic and a little salt to taste, and you'll have yourself a tasty fish stock to enhance any fish sauce or soup.

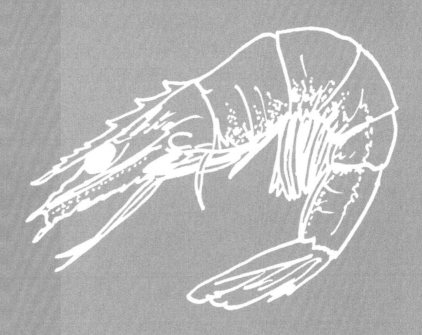

Bristol Athletic Football Club

"From the pot, fish bubbling
in the kitchen,
giving off the
scent that reminds
me of the beach.
On the plate a fascinating
array of provisions all
shapes, and textures,
topped with the
'fruits de mer:
That's 'fruit of the sea',
filled with offensive
weapons: that's bones to
you and me."

Taken from 'Caribbean Moments' by Sherrie Eugene-Hart

Seafood

IT'S EASTER. GOOD FRIDAY IS the day dedicated to fish! Fried red snapper is a perfect choice and a real treat. Heads on or off, it really doesn't matter just be careful of the bones. SERVES 4

Fried Snapper and Vinaigrette Onions

4 red snapper (gutted and scaled)
2 tbs fish seasoning OR fish masala
3 large garlic cloves chopped

1 tsp coarse black pepper
1 lemon
Splash of oil for marinade
Oil for frying

Plain flour for coating fish before frying

For the garnish

Bunch of coriander
1 onion sliced in rings
Splash of vinegar

1 red sweet pepper sliced in rings
Sprinkle of all-purpose seasoning

Fresh lemon/lime quarters to garnish

1 Wash the gutted fish, cut off fins and slice the flesh twice on each side. (Remove eyes optional. Eyes are a delicacy in some Caribbean islands.)

2 Smother with lemon juice, fish seasoning, garlic, oil, vinegar and black pepper both inside and out and leave to marinade for at least an hour.

3 Coat each fish with plain flour.

4 Heat the oil and fry fish for at least 5 minutes on each side.

5 After all the fish has been fried, keep warm in oven.

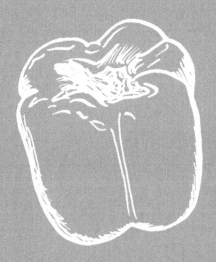

Vinaigrette onions

1. Shallow fry onions, pepper, vinegar, all purpose seasoning for about 3 minutes. Add fresh coriander, and smother over the fish. Use fresh cut lemon or lime to garnish. Serve hot or cold.

Tip Feel free to keep the fish whole or cut into two or three. Snapper bones are really hard so be careful. It may be wise to use filleted fish.

THIS FISHY SNACK HAS RITA written all over it. As children, we knew we were in for salt fish fritters when the house completely stunk of boiled salt fish that lingered in the house for days. Mum was quite famous for her salt fish fritters, selling them at festivals all over Bristol. If you're from Dominica you'll know the correct name for salt fish fritters and dumpling is Acra and Jonny Cake.

Carib-Asian Fish Fritters and Dumplings

1 pack of salt fish (boiled in water to remove the salt)
4 garlic cloves

1 red chilli
Handful of coriander
1 tbs fish seasoning

1 tbs curry powder
Few sprigs of fresh thyme

Method for Fritters

1 Blend together the onion, garlic, chilli and coriander.

2 Remove from the blender and add the salt fish.

3 Add one cup of water to the mixture, together with the fish seasoning curry powder and flour.

4 Mix the batter thoroughly. Make sure the constancy is not too thin and not as thick as clotted cream.

5 Spoon into in hot oil. Make 4 or 5 at one time and flip over until golden brown on each side.

Method for the Dumplings

1 Mix the flour, water and pinch of salt together. Kneed like bread and divide into UFO-shaped circles. Fry in hot oil until golden brown.

 Serve fritter and dumpling and salad garnish with raita and a hot pepper sauce.

WE LOVE EXPERIMENTING. WE TRIED this recipe for the first time on camera. Thank goodness it worked! Tuna will never be the same again. **SERVES 4**

Mango and Lime-Infused Tuna

4 chunky tuna steaks
Juice from 3 limes
1 large mango diced
1 onion finely chopped

3 cloves of garlic
1 tbs fish seasoning
1 tbs black pepper
1 tsp mixed herbs

1 tsp of lime and coriander
seasoning powder

1   Wash the fish and season in a large bowl.

2   Using the juice from 1 lime, half tsp of fish seasoning, half tsp black pepper, lime and coriander seasoning and the mixed herbs, make a marinade for the fish. Set aside for at least 15 minutes while the fish takes in the flavour.

3   Heat a large frying pan add the oil and fry the onions, garlic and mango.

4   Add the remaining fish seasoning and black pepper.

5   When the onions are soft, add the fish and saute for a few minutes.

6   Turn the fish and add the remaining lime towards the end of cooking. The cooking process should take about 7 minutes in total. Garnish with coriander and serve with rice and salad.

 Tip   Be careful as you turn the tuna as it is likely to break up.

ACKEE IS THE NATIONAL FOOD of Jamaica and has a delicate and delightful taste. It's an ideal breakfast dish or part of a wholesome supper. We've teamed it up with paratha, forming a perfect Carib-Asian fusion. **SERVES 6**

Ackee and Salt Fish on Paratha

Tin of ackee
Packet of filleted salt fish (salt already boiled out)
1 large onion chopped
5 cloves garlic finely chopped
Handful of fresh thyme

Handful of fresh coriander
3 tomatoes sliced
1 Scotch bonnet pepper seeded and chopped
1 tsp fish seasoning
½ tsp coarse black pepper

1 tsp all-purpose seasoning
Splash of oyster sauce
Generous splash of olive oil
6 ready-made parathas

1   Flake the salt fish.

2   Heat pan and fry onions, garlic, and thyme until soft.

3   Add Scotch bonnet pepper, fish seasoning, all-purpose seasoning, half the coriander and the salt fish and cook through.

4   Add a little more olive oil if it starts to dry.

5   Finally add the oyster sauce and gently fold in the ackee (and half the water) and sprinkle on your black pepper.

6   Cook for a few more minutes to warm the ackee through, being careful not to mash the ackee.

7   Simmer on a low heat for about 3 minutes.

8   Serve on warm parathas and garnish with fresh tomatoes and the remaining fresh coriander.

 Tip You can use Jamaican hard dough bread, naan bread or chapati bread with this dish. Also the Scotch bonnet pepper is very hot. It is extra hot with the seeds. Use red capsicum pepper for colour if you prefer as it's not hot at all.

HERE'S ANOTHER ONE OF THOSE dishes that will make you want more. Brilliant finger food as part of a buffet or a tasty treat day or night. You'll love it either way.

Snapper and Sweet Potato Fish Cakes

4 filleted and cooked snapper fish (poach in salt water)
4 sweet potatoes mashed
3 large Irish potatoes mashed
1 large onion finely chopped

Small handful of dill chopped (save some for garnish)
1 tbs garlic granules
1 tsp fish masala
1 tbs ground coriander

½ tsp chilli flakes
½ tsp cumin seeds
2 eggs whipped
Bread crumbs
Oil for frying

1 In a large bowl, mix together the sweet and Irish potato until smooth. Use a little milk and knob of butter if you want to.

2 Add the snapper fish flakes, onions, dill, garlic granules, fish masala, coriander, chilli flakes and cumin seeds.

3 Mix well. The consistency should be stiff, like mash!

4 Using your hands, form the potato into circles or dumpling shapes.

5 Brush each one with egg wash and coat each with breadcrumbs.

6 In a large pan, shallow fry the fishcakes until brown on each side (use a medium heat so the breadcrumbs don't burn).

7 Serve with a chilli dip and salad.

 Tip Use any filleted fish of your choice. Salmon works particularly well. Raita dip instead of chilli dip works well too. You can finish the fishcakes off in the oven.

"This is a poem to all the music lovers
        To every race across the world
my sisters and brothers."

Taken from 'A Poem' – Freshblood Crew – *The Definitive Freshblood Collection* – Freshblood Records

"I am recruiting so when the power comes to me I'll be reigning maybe even forcibly Keeping it fair I know I'll see the day that separatist views won't ever get no leeway I'm not a racist proof is in my colour, black or white can't dominate each other With a kick punch or gun I don't believe that black is the better or white is up higher Live Your Life in honesty."

Taken from 'Live Your Life In Honesty' – Freshblood Crew – *The Definitive Freshblood Collection* – Freshblood Records

THIS DISH IS A PERSONAL favourite! Don't worry about knives, forks, accompaniments or company! Be selfish and treat yourself to this shellfish indulgence (or at least put an extra portion back for later when you're alone). SERVES 4

Chilli King Prawn Special

20 fresh king prawns with shell on
3 green chillis
Two large onions finely chopped
2 cloves

4 or 5 garlic cloves finely chopped
2 cloves
Sprigs of dry thyme
2 star anise

1 tsp allspice seeds
4 cardamom pods
3 tbs oyster sauce
2 tbs brown sugar
Splash of olive oil

1 Using a pestle and mortar, crush the allspice, star anise, cardamoms, cloves and dry thyme.

2 In a large frying pan, dry cook the spices until they release their aromas. Be careful not to burn them.

3 Add a splash of olive oil together with your onions, chillis, garlic and brown sugar. Cook through.

4 Take the intestine out of the prawns by slicing through the back of the shell and washing it out.

5 Add the prawns to the onion and mix through.

6 Finally use a generous splash of oyster sauce (we've suggested 3 tablespoons) and continue cooking for at least 2 minutes. Serve immediately.

 Tip Feel free to use already-cooked king prawns. They will be pink.

IT'S A MEATY FISH THAT lends itself perfectly to a healthy light curry dish that's ideal for lunch or dinner. **SERVES 4 LARGE PORTIONS**

Coley Curry

1lb coley chopped into bite-sized pieces (with the central bone)
3 spring onions chopped
1 yellow capsicum pepper chopped

¼ small white cabbage chopped
4 garlic cloves
1 ½ tbs garam masala
1 ½ tbs fish seasoning
1 ½ tbs curry powder

½ tsp black pepper
1 tin of tomatoes
Splash of olive oil
Handful of coriander for seasoning and garnish

1 Wash the coley and sprinkle with lemon juice.

2 Season with 1 tbs garam masala, 1 tbs fish seasoning, 1 tbs curry powder, ½ tsp black pepper and half of your chopped coriander. Set aside.

3 In a frying pan, heat your oil and fry your spring onions, garlic, red capsicum pepper and cabbage.

4 Now include the remainder of your seasoning and stir until the vegetables are soft.

5 Add the tomatoes and get the mixture to bubbling point.

6 Add the fish and turn down the heat. Simmer for 20 minutes. Your coley curry is ready!

Tip Serve with rice. Don't stir the curry too vigorously as it may flake. Use fish that is meaty like monkfish or even lobster. On another day substitute the tinned tomato with a tin of coconut milk to make coley and coconut curry.

HERE'S ANOTHER DISH THAT WE advise you to eat with people you know very well. You'll need your fingers, a bib and no inhibitions. **SERVES 4**

Crab Claw and Coconut Curry

2 crabs (already prepared and cooked crab meat, crack the crab claws for easy access to the meat)
1 large onion chopped
4 garlic cloves

1 Scotch bonnet (whole)
Sprigs of thyme
1 tbs fish seasoning
1 tsp turmeric
1 tbs curry powder
Juice from 1 lemon

Splash of fish sauce
Splash of olive oil
1 tin of coconut
1 spring onion chopped for the garnish

1 Season the crab with lemon juice, fish seasoning and thyme. Splash a bit of olive oil in there too. Set aside.

2 In a hot pan, fry the onions, garlic and whole Scotch bonnet pepper.

3 Add in the turmeric, curry powder, and a little more fish seasoning.

4 Add the tin of coconut milk and stir.

5 After a few minutes add the crab meat and claws and simmer until warmed through.

6 Garnish with spring onion and serve with rice.

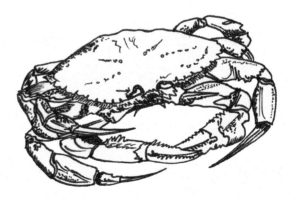

 This dish should take you about 30 minutes to cook. You will need a suitable utensil to prise the meat out of the crab claws, otherwise you've wasted the appeal (and the meat) of this mouthwatering dish.

WE BOTH HAVE THE EXPERIENCE of being brought up in the UK so fish and chips is as normal and as appealing as a good spicy bolognaise. But we don't class this next recipe as normal. The fish is monkfish and the chips are sweet. See what you think. **SERVES 6**

Carib-Asian Fish and Chips

Fillets from 2 monkfish
1 tbs fish masala
Juice from 1 lemon

For the batter

1 cup plain flour
1 cup gram flour
2 cups lager (or ginger beer)

For the chips

5 large sweet potatoes (peeled and chipped)

1 Season the monkfish fillets with fish masala and lemon juice. Set aside.

2 To make the batter, simply pour the beer into a bowl with the flour and a little fish masala, and stir until the consistency is smooth and flowing. Add more beer or flour to get the consistency right. Set aside while you prepare the chips.

3 In a chip pan or a frying pan, fry the sweet potato chips in hot oil until golden brown all over over. Keep in a warm oven.

4 Make sure your oil is hot enough to fry the fish.

5 Dip your fillet monkfish into the batter and place into the deep fryer until golden brown all over. Serve your fish and chips hot.

 Serve with a fusion of ketchup and hot pepper sauce if you can handle it.

THIS IS A GREAT SHOWSTOPPER centre piece and a lovely way to eat together around the table. Any large fish could work and almost any filling of choice. **SERVES 8 GENEROUS PORTIONS**

Stuffed Tilapia Fish

Large tilapia gutted and gilled (keep head on optional)
4 limes (two for the juice and two for the garnish)
5 garlic cloves mashed

Bunch of dill for seasoning and and garnish
Bunch of coriander for seasoning and garnish
1 tbs fish masala

Splash of fish sauce
Splash of olive oil
Parchment paper or foil to wrap fish

For the Stuffing

Two cups of pre-cooked rice
Small tin of corn
2 spring onions

One red capsicum pepper chopped
Chopped dill

1 green chilli pepper finely chopped

Method for the fish

1 Wash the fish and smother with lime juice.

2 Make 2 or 3 cuts into each side.

3 In a baking tray, place your parchment paper or foil (enough to wrap around the fish) and sprinkle with a little olive oil. Then place the dill, coriander, 2 crushed garlic cloves, a sprinkling of fish masala and a splash of fish sauce on your tin.

4 Season the fish inside and out with the remaining seasoning. Be sure to season inside the slits. Place the fish in the tin, and put the oven on gas mark 6.

Method for the filling

1. Fry your spring onions, garlic and chilli together with the remaining seasoning.

2. Add your cooked rice. Mix for a few minutes and leave to cool.

3. Spoon the cooled filling into the fish. It's fine if it overflows.

4. Finally splash the fish with olive oil, lime juice and dill.

5. Gently fold over the parchment paper or foil over the fish and place in a preheated oven.

6. Bake for 35–40 minutes.

7. Garnish with dill, coriander and lime slices.

 Tip Smaller fish will require less cooking time.

"Now maybe I'm just a fool but I'm
still wondering why
The hell I get so upset that
people even don't try
To repay some of the love that's
always given their way
And just acknowledge the fact
maybe they'll need you someday
Not for material things or for
financial gain
I'm talking caring for
friendship and easing the pain so
you will recognise love
and how it's passed onto you
And just accept it with warmth
without needing a clue."

Taken from – 'You & I' Freshblood Feat Dan Ratchet – *The Definitive Freshblood Collection* – *Freshblood Records*

VEGETARIAN AND VEGAN DISHES. It's the bit in the book as a child I'd skip past. No meat usually meant boring and incomplete. These prejudices would spill out onto the people who were vegan or vegetarian, describing them as 'hippyish', or 'brown-sandal people'. We've come to realise that so much of our food is so versatile and creative, just like the people around us. Everyone is valuable and all food has potential.

We always bang on about being different and experimenting with your food and this section is no exception.

Many years ago I presented a vegetarian cookery programme called *Green Grow the Dishes*.

Although it was a great experience, I managed to get through the whole series without the use of serious spice flavours. Not my call. At last, I can stamp my spicy mark on this vegetarian and vegan food collection.

You can use these dishes as full meals, snacks or side dishes either way. Veggies and vegans out there, this is for you!

Grow Your Own

DAD HAD AN ALLOTMENT. It was situated in beautiful green surroundings with a river that was home to sticklebacks. Being a tomboy who loved the great outdoors, this environment was paradise. I loved running, playing football and fishing. Dad would be in his element gardening and I fishing with sister Judy.

When we were hungry we'd find Dad, who'd be digging horse manure into the soil. He would leave that task, wash his hands and then dig for carrots with his bare hands. After cleaning them and giving us two each, he'd send us back fishing with a smile on his face, satisfied that we were fed.

I DON'T KNOW WHY BUT even as a youngster I associated vegetarian food with health and performance, and I still do.

Of course, the rise of Jamaican athletes on the track has highlighted even more the benefits of 'provisions' from the islands and this ideology is further illustrated by many of the football players I've managed and played alongside who have eaten healthy fruit and vegetables before and after games (I'm not saying we never eat burgers, though). My time with Bristol Athletic Football Club saw some memorable victories in the UK, Holland and Spain. It also helped me to realise the advantages of fruit and exciting vegetarian dishes that use spice and celebrated ingredients that have known health benefits, like turmeric. Of course, much Asian food is vegetarian anyway, and the Rastafarian Ital diet is vegan.

The things you would learn if you were part of a mixed team or group like my football club! Often Sherrie and my mum would volunteer to cook at the fundraising events for the club and it wasn't surprising that their dishes were normally sold out.

"It doesn't matter if you come
from St Pauls, St Werbs or Easton,
Kingswood, Clifton or Bishopston.
Matters not if you wear
a salwar kameez. In some schools
that's a no no.
My A star friend wears a kimono.
With pride. No time to hide.
Wear your sari, wrap, *Turban* or *Topi*
and hold your head high
for you and for me.
It doesn't matter if yam and dasheen
is your meal or bammy or madras
feel good about your
Irish stew and love your
peas and mash."

Taken from 'School Day Memories' by Sherrie Eugene-Hart

Vegetarian

WE ALL KNOW THE TRADITIONAL coleslaw that so often ends up as a side dish with both English and Caribbean food, but there are alternatives too that can prove a real compliment to many of the recipes in our book.

Beetroot and White Radish Slaw

2 large white radishes grated
3 raw beetroots grated
1 onion grated
For the dressing

4 cloves of crushed garlic
1/3 cup of olive oil
Juice from half squeezed lemon
Large splash of vinegar

1 tbs brown sugar
Pinch of salt

1 Mix the radish, beetroot and onion together.

2 In a separate bowl, mix the crushed garlic, oil, vinegar, sugar and pinch of salt.

3 Warm in the microwave for 40 seconds or until the brown sugar has disintegrated.

4 Pour over the carrot and beetroot, mix through and serve when ready.

 Tip If you wanted to, you could substitute the dressing for mayo, and use carrot instead of radish. It works just as well. Serve with yam sag aloo and rice.

THIS IS A GREAT SNACK to cook while your guests are waiting for their meals. It's a great talking point and pretty much any veg works well. A brilliant appetizer too.

Veggie Bujias

1 onion sliced
Cauliflower florets
1 courgette sliced or shredded
2 potatoes cooked and diced
Bunch of spinach

½ tsp cumin seeds
½ tsp black pepper
1 tsp garam masala
2 chilli peppers chopped
3 garlic cloves chopped

Small handful of chopped coriander
Oil for shallow frying

For the batter

3 cups gram flour
2 cups water

1 Start with the batter. In a large bowl put your gram flour and mix in your water, cumin seeds, garam masala and black pepper. The batter should be the consistency of custard.

2 Add your vegetables including chilli, garlic and coriander and mix.

3 In a large pan of hot oil spoon your bujas into the pan until they are golden brown on each side.

 Tip Taste the first bujia to make sure you are happy with the taste. Add more seasoning if you need to.

THIS FRESH VEG DISH IS so good-looking! What strikes us most are the colours; they go so well together and are very impressive for a dinner party.

Fusion Cabbage

Half purple cabbage sliced
Half white cabbage sliced
4 large carrots halved

Bunch of spinach
Tsp black pepper
Tsp seasoning salt

2 garlic cloves whole
1 star anise
Splash of olive oil

1   Place your garlic cloves, a pinch of black pepper, a pinch of seasoning salt, carrots and star anise in a shallow pan of boiling water.

2   After 5 minutes, add your white cabbage.

3   Meanwhile, cook your purple cabbage separately so that it doesn't discolour the other food. Add your seasoning of salt and pepper to this too.

4   Towards the end of cooking (when the carrots are soft) add the spinach to the mix. It will become limp very quickly.

5   Finally assemble your veg creatively in your way. Sprinkle with olive oil. Serve hot.

Tip Use other veg like pumpkin or artichoke if you like the look and taste.

EVEN THOUGH THIS WASN'T A dish that was cooked at home, saag aloo was always ordered when we ate at an Indian restaurant. Spinach and potato the perfect side alongside rice and salad. What better than to add yam to this dish. It fits perfectly and its addition makes it a meal on its own. **SERVES 6**

Yam Saag Aloo

1lb yam or edows
1lb potatoes
1 bunch spinach or callaloo
1 onion chopped

3 garlic cloves chopped
1 tbs garam masala
1 tsp chilli flakes
1 star anise

Splash of olive oil
1 maggi cube

1 Peel and dice your yam and potatoes and boil with a maggi cube until soft (but not mashed) and set aside.

2 Fry your onions, garlic, chilli flakes, masala, cumin seeds and star anise. Mix together until the onions are soft. You may need to add a little more olive oil.

3 Add the spinach and cook until it wilts.

4 Add the yam and potatoes together with a little of the stock and gently fold in. Be careful not to mash the potato and yam too much.

5 Garnish with coriander.

 Tip Goes nicely with rice and peas. Use sweet potato instead of Irish potato for a change and save the stock from the yam and potato for soup.

I COULD EAT THIS ALL day every day! At home this would be our staple meal with rice. One bowl full was never enough and there was always some left in the pan. I defy anyone to ask where the meat is when you try this. I promise you, you will NOT miss it. In fact, apologies for using the M-word. **SERVES 4–6 GENEROUS PORTIONS**

Daal and Dumplings

3 cups of yellow lentils soaked for a couple hours
1 onion
2 red chillies chopped
2 garlic cloves chopped
Thumb size of ginger chopped (or

tbs ground ginger)
1 tsp curry powder
1 tsp all-purpose seasoning
2 bay leaves
2 cloves
5 pimentos

1 tsp mustard seeds
5 spring onions finely chopped
2 garlic cloves chopped
Handful of Coriander leaves (save some for the garnish)

1 In a large pan, boil up the lentils, garlic, bay leaf, curry powder and all-purpose seasoning. Cook lentils until soft but not disintegrated. This should take about an hour. Drain and add a tin of chopped tomatoes. Cook through and set aside.

2 In a pestle and mortar, grind down the cloves, pimentos, mustard seeds, spring onions, garlic and a little coriander. Add a little olive oil. It will resemble a lumpy paste.

3 Fry the grinded mixture for a few minutes then add it to the lentils and mix through. Cook for a further three minutes or so on medium heat. Careful not to catch it. Stir.

4 Garnish with the remaining coriander leaves. Serve hot!

For dumplings see the Fish Fritters and Dumplings recipe on page 90.

Tip

Serve with rice and chappati, or just with dumplings. There are a huge variety of lentils out there. Try them all. Also use fresh tomatoes instead of tinned ones if your prefer, and to add a luxurious taste and texture why not add a couple of tablespoons of butter?

RICE! LOVE IT OR HATE IT, many dishes need it! I'm talking about the cooking of it, of course, not the taste. We both have a phobia about cooking rice, but usually Sherrie can pull it off by accident. At home we have now succumbed to a rice cooker but go on, give our recipe a try. SERVES 4–6

Pumpkin Rice

Three cups of basmati rice washed
2 tbs biryani mix

Half a pumpkin peeled and chopped
1 onion finely chopped

Finger size piece of cinnamon
Splash of vegetable oil
Coriander to garnish

1 Fry the onion and pumpkin together with the biryani mix and cinnamon stick in a little oil on medium heat.

2 Add the rice, mix and cover with two cups of water. Make sure it covers the rice. Put a lid on and lower the heat.

3 Cook for about 15 mins until all the water has evaporated.

4 Garnish with coriander.

THIS ICONIC DISH IS A real pleaser. The rice should take the colour of the peas, which are, in fact, beans, truth be known. Aunty Min has the best recipe of all. This is our version and it really is as delicious as Aunty Min's. SERVES 4–6 GENEROUS PORTIONS

Rice and Peas

3 cups of basmati rice washed
3 cups kidney beans soaked in cold water overnight
5 twigs of fresh thyme

2 garlic cloves whole
1 finger of cinnamon stick
1 tin of coconut milk
1 tsp all-purpose seasoning

Splash of oil

1   Boil your soaked beans until soft. This should take about an hour.

2   In the meantime, fry your cinnamon stick, thyme, garlic and spring onions.

3   Add all-purpose seasoning.

4   Stir in your rice, followed by coconut milk and beans (including enough bean water to cover the rice by about an inch).

5   Put a lid on and cook on a regular heat until the liquid has evaporated. This should take about 15–20 minutes. Lower the heat or even turn it off at the end of cooking. This will allow the rice to steam.

Tip Serve with yam saag aloo.

YES THEY LOOK LIKE BANANAS, but they're not! They are generally larger and must be cooked first. Green or ripe, they're a welcome addition to savoury dishes. And, just in case you were wondering, it's 'plantin' not 'plaintain' as the spelling suggests. **SERVES 3–4**

Fried Plantain

2 ripe plantains
Vegetable oil for frying

1   Peel the plantain.

2   Slice them diagonally into thin slices.

3   Fry in hot oil until golden brown on each side.

4   Use kitchen roll to soak the excess oil.

Tip Don't be put off by the black dots on the plantain. This is because they are ripe and sweet. In fact the darker the sweeter. Serve on its own or as part of a meal. Either way they're seriously yummy!

LET'S BE HONEST, WE RARELY make our own chapatis, yet we love them so much. There are so many local stores that sell authentic chapatis, naans, parathas and rotis so we spoil ourselves. However, they go with almost everything in our book, and once you get a feel for bread like this we reckon you'll be making them all the time. It's best to use chapati flour, which you can get from most supermarkets or better still from your local Asian or Caribbean store as they make a softer chapati.

Chapati

2 cups chapati flour
(or 1 cup wholemeal & 1 cup of plain flour)

Pinch of salt
Cup of water

3 tbs vegetable oil or melted butter

1   In a mixing bowl sift in the flour and salt.

2   Make a well and gradually pour in the water and mix with your hands until you've formed a dough.

3   Kneed for about 3 minutes and divide into roughly 10 balls. The longer you knead the dough the softer your chapatis will be.

4   On a floured surface roll out each dough ball. Use the flour to to stop them from sticking in a pile.

5   Heat a frying pan with a little oil and place one onto it.

6   When it starts blistering gently fry the other side.

7   Brush the bread with butter or olive oil on each side. They will be soft yet crunchy in part.

8   Wrap the chapatis in a clean tea towel until you've completed.

"Our Recipes and Rhymes
we hope have
blended together
for you
like Yam Saag Aloo
or Ackee and
Chapati."

WHETHER YOU USE THIS BOOK to savour the pictures, muse over the rhymes or to cook your favorite dishes, we hope there has been something here for you that has made you smile and perhaps resonated with your own life.

We would like to think that you have come away with sense of accomplishment, belonging, pride and understanding, sentiments that we hope transcend far beyond food but into the rich kaleidoscope of cultural diversity and human harmony. We can't change the world but perhaps we can change what people think about each other, just one dish at a time.

Epilogue

OUR CARIBBEAN AND ASIAN ROOTS and our love for humanity and what we eat have brought us to this point. With everything that's going on in the world today, we truly believe that food is a great leveler. From fine dining to outdoor bush-style treats, it's a way of getting people talking, laughing and learning.

Writing this book has reminded us of the little gems we experienced as children growing up in our large families:

Me, Sherrie, in our quarry-tiled kitchen in St Werburgh's, watching mum wash the tripe and add it in the soup, which was to become our God-sent nourishment for the next two days.

And me, Pat, watching in awe as mum made my favourite, daal and rice, as she marvelled over the spices readily available in Asian stores. Shopping here was like shopping for diamonds.

Our first book is just a taste of things to come. As we continue to explore our fusion taste buds and experiment with cultural ideas we will always remain true to the origins of our Carib-Asian roots. Whilst acknowledging the amazing influences of French, African, Portuguese and, of course, British food in our cooking, we will always have our mums, (and dads), inspiration at the heart of it.

Acknowledgements

SPECIAL LOVE AND THANKS TO our parents Rita and Hector Eugene and Ruth and John Hart.

A hearty warm thanks to all the people who've helped us along the way during the production of this book.

Errol Ballin BRB Caribbean Food Store
Yousef Mohammed – Kashmir Butchers
Tovey's Sea Food
Mr Singh SSA World of Spice
Sweet Mart
Malik Supermarket Easton
Alnoor Supermarket
Mr Rajani - Rajani's Superstore
Mam Seedy Neephi Foods
Made TV
Bristol
Cardiff
Tyne and Wear
Leeds
Chris James
Steve Richmond
Big Center TV Birmingham
Bay TV Liverpool

Latest TV Brighton
8th Sense Media
e-com Media

Jamie Meacham
Tom Hines
Jack Rebours
Tom Rochelle
Mike Jenkins
Michael Benjamin St Louis
Charlie Dunrod

Robin Morgan
Marie Brock
Sangeeta Devan
Sarah Molden
Suzi Purdie
Victoria Tiley
Mackenzie Hanifan
Shelena Artman
Courtney Henry
Memona Taras - Mughal Emporium
Kate Gander
Vince Gander
Jamaar Semper-House
Minette Semper
Rob Collins - Duke Box Beats
Dan Ratchet
Plaster PR
Kellie
Dani
Beryl
BCfm Radio
Watershed

Christina Robino
Bristol Central Youth FC
Catherine Farina -The Chefs Forum

Special thanks to John Hart (Dad), Summer, Solomon Shelena, India and Tevez for putting up with a kitchen full of cameras!

Index of Recipes